Apperception

Apperception

Emily Bilman

Copyright © Emily Bilman 2020

The moral right of the author has been asserted.

Apart from any fair dealing for the purposes of research or private study, or criticism or review, as permitted under the Copyright, Designs and Patents Act 1988, this publication may only be reproduced, stored or transmitted, in any form or by any means, with the prior permission in writing of the publishers and the author and, in the case of reprographic reproduction in accordance with the terms of licences issued by the Copyright Licensing Agency. Enquiries concerning reproduction outside those terms should be sent to the publishers and the author. All other inquiries should be sent to the author.

Matador
9 Priory Business Park,
Wistow Road, Kibworth Beauchamp,
Leicestershire. LE8 0RX
Tel: 0116 279 2299
Email: books@troubador.co.uk
Web: www.troubador.co.uk/matador
Twitter: @matadorbooks

ISBN 978 1800461 031

British Library Cataloguing in Publication Data.
A catalogue record for this book is available from the British Library.

Printed and bound in the UK by TJ International, Padstow, Cornwall
Typeset in 13pt Aldine by Troubador Publishing Ltd, Leicester, UK

Matador is an imprint of Troubador Publishing Ltd

Contents

APPERCEPTION	1
Apperception	3
The Life-Buoy and The Blackbird	4
Vigilance	5
Ultrasound	6
The Child With The Prism	7
Initiation	8
Fodder	9
Cleaved	10
Fluctuations	11
The Water-Shadow	12
The Water-Shadow	13
The Torn Tower	14
Fallen Icarus	15
Thresholds	16
THE ARMED POET	17
The Armed Poet	19
The Virtual Child	20
Love's Reply	21
Introspection	22
Art	23
Suture	24
The Bee's Sting	25
Ode to Sleep	26
QUARANTINE	28
Protest	29
Quarantine	30
Covid-19	31
Counterpoint	32
The Gin Epidemic, 1751	33
Tatters	34
Time's Disintegration	35
The Stages of Cruelty – 1751 & 2020	36
Foxes	37

The Fox	38
Crows and Quills	39
Memorabilia	40
The Bell	41
Self-shielded	42
The Trapped Rake	43
The Rake's Quarantine	44
THE DREAM-MASK	45
Darkness Revisited	47
The Dream-Mask	48
The Dream-Shadow	49
The Eastern Façade	50
The Hawk's Prey	51
Trammel	52
Triassic Gifts	53
On the mountain	54
The Ascent	55
Transience	56
Pentimento	57
The Dream Cadence	58
INSCAPE	59
Inscape	61
The Scantling	62
The Blood-Pearl	63
On the Causeway	64
Birthright	65
Transformations	66
Self-image	67
The Olive Branch	68
The Minotaur-Daughter	69
The Minotaur-Daughter	70
Epithalamium	71
Rebellion With An Actor and A Poet	72
Water On Water	73
The New Order	75
The Clash of Contraries	76
Acknowledgements	79
Author's Biography	82

Apperception

Apperception

The interferometer that chronicled terrains
in *relief*, conceded mapping the ignorant anger,
empathy, pity, and impotence I had felt
as a young girl, when you, father, were
harshly threatened by exclusion.
The letter I wrote you on the boat
travelling to the Aegean island remained
unachieved due to high seas. I remember
writing the letter while waves surged into a storm
thinking of you and my grandmother,
a tall Caucasian lady, who kept black
moleskin journals in her own language.
Our close bond kept me in the security of home.
The boat journey turned out to be as unsettling
as my fugues' fantasized mutability.
Like the currents that moved the seas,
the letter was again amended when my son
suffered trauma as a fugue-child
and we re-located to a foreign city.
The letter that brought the passengers
safely to the port outside the capital, father,
remains lost. Ironically, my architect boyfriend
whom you had met presaged I would become
a lay-astronomer. The telescope, father,
tempered my apperception.

The Life-Buoy and The Blackbird

The stranded skies of my childhood
Were streaked with an erratic anguish
As if I were lost in an unfamiliar circus
Where uncanny clowns jounced and shuffled
While subdued animals performed acrobatics
In a hermetic circus-tent shut to the world.

Like a furless animal on a tumultuous day,
I clung to my father's outstretched hand
Raising me beyond my anxious fear
Like a life-buoy thrown on stormy seas.

The next day, the wind's breaths refreshed
The garden, stretching it towards the horizon
While the blackbird sang a larkspurs' tune
And the foxgloves aspired to the azure.

Vigilance

In the resilient haze of my infanthood
A half-opened drawer of linens
Exuded my mother's fragrance
Mixed with almond, and cloves.

Cradled by a new-born glossolalia
Steeped in the dreamscape
Of plankton-strewn seas, I withstood
Temporary emptiness.

Like a passage of truth in a book
Igniting my vigilance
Sustenance atoned my hunger
Initiating new-born speech.

Ultrasound

As the echo-graph slid on my skin
Tautened by new life, I thought of the poet's
Insight that the child is father to man.
On the chiaroscuro screen, I saw my baby's
Body oscillate like a kelp forest through oceanic
Currents carrying plankton to the sea-depths.
The symmetry of his heart beat now recurs
In my poem's rhythm like an undertow.
With the symmetry of his heart-beat
I imagine schools of dolphins echo-locating
With rhythms resonating in the sea-depths.

The Child With The Prism

Red for the apples and orange for the oranges
Yellow for the canaries that tread on the grass
Evergreen firs stretching beyond the house
Robins that sing in violet, blue, and indigo.
Out in the garden, the child realizes the prism
Refracts the light in his hands into rainbows.
He, then, hides in the shadow of the lime tree
Tries to catch the light on the glass triangle
But the rainbow seems as pale as sand.
The shade waned the iridescence as if to reproach
Him selfishness, temper tantrums, his protean
Whims. Pensive, he places the prism in sunlight

Enthused to behold the rainbow's rebirth
As when the rain cleans the tilled earth.

Initiation

You said the taste of the salmon eggs
On toast remained in your mouth

After we parted. You said you missed me.
A month later, you were forever gone.

You died suddenly like the juvenile fox
You gunned down in our nocturnal garden.

After your death my muteness increased
The lead-silence that invaded our house.

While the sky turned crimson and pewter-grey
The doves flew off from the scented bower.

Your absence felt like a broken metaphor whose
Figure of weakness was devoid of its vehicle.

Yet, the shadow of your ghost constantly
Remained with me like a husband in waiting.

As I journeyed towards Ithaca, unafraid
Like Ulysses, to confront the rough seas

I unravelled my secret quest of self-discovery
Deeper than the deepest ocean trench, a quest

Which sustained me like the lustrous salmon
Eggs we ate during our last meal together.

Fodder

His other self milked the ewe
on the meadow in the spring
of their contentment.

The lovers roamed right above
the town's rooftops patterned
in uneven tiled geometries.

With the greenness of his mind
he offered clover, grain and grass
to the sheep in the pasture.

His other self watched as if
a bond of blood united them
while the fodder turned to milk.

Cleaved

They felt the rhythm of their bodies as they tilled
Turned, raked, aired, and composted the soil
And planted tobacco, cotton, corn or coffee.

Erect or bent, their bodies recollected the land's rhythms
The corn or coffee they harvested, erect or bent,
The impossibility of abandoning the gleaned harvest.

Day after day, they carried out their work's yolk.
At night, they remembered and the next day sang
The rhythms of the new harvests they collected.

Their bodies remembered the rhythms of their native
Lands improvised into grassroots jazz and blues.
The land's rhythms shaped the blues they sang.

Tied to the land they could not abandon, its rhythms
Became the melancholy of their forgotten freedom
Until the land's rent war-cry freed their cleaved bodies.

Fluctuations

Would melancholy submerge me like a black tide
If suddenly the earth were to swallow the seas?

Without the sea's light, I would be blinded
In my room by the sun-bleached window panes.

I would no longer feel my body as weightless
As sea-water fresh as mint-lemon on my mouth.

I would no longer rise from my bed in the morning
With the sea's bittersweet smell of brine and iodine

Daylight would not be diffused like a silk drapery
Undulating on the beryl-beach where children shape

The patient sand with ephemeral castles
With the resolute scrutiny of sculptors.

By the sea, I daydream with the waves' motion
While the sea breeze intimates a subtle rhythm.

Poetry, like supple plankton, vacillates forever.

The Water-Shadow

When I make my first steps into
the wide sea and a swarm of juvenile
gilt-breams swirl around my legs
I linger on the brink of the beryl-beach
like an infatuated maiden of the moon.
My feet submerged in salt-water
I sense the soft skins of the breams
and rejoice in their silver transparencies.

As I swim I suddenly feel
frightened by my own shadow
beneath me as if it were the shadow
of a wild thief possessing me
or the unknown shadows of multitudes
threatening my communion
with the nurturing salt-water
that bore me as a child.

The Water-Shadow

The gilt-breams still slide
on the diaphanous waters,
their lithe dorsal fins bent down
like folded sails while I dive
head-down into the salt-water,
blessing each mineral ion oozing
into my skin, carrying me into
the depths, rendering me weightless.

While I swim back towards the shore
the gilt-breams slither along the breaths
of the soft sea-sands, their spines
secretly clasping their silver-shaded lamella
blending in their own transparencies
their crimson phosphorescent
gills, pumping mineral oxygen
like a marine heart bitter to the taste.

The Torn Tower

Fireflies shone under the hydrangeas
until, gradually, the glow-spots grew countless
like the stars in the clear nocturnal sky.
Their incandescence enchanted me

during my evening meal of grilled fish
sprinkled with olive oil and lemon juice.
Some sweet lettuce leaves were chewed
by myriad leech-teeth when the caterers

started to carry away the tray with the wine
and the superposed plates like the fireflies
on the slime-soil soaked with iodine, all too glad

to get their tips for their prospects as they traversed
the iron-wrought gates leading to the open sea
boundless except for a torn tower on a promontory.

Fallen Icarus

Like an epic hero
Daedalus hugged his son as both
left the labyrinth

Janus-like, father
and son reflected each other
under the sun-kiln

Icarus dared to fly.
A whirlpool oozed his body
in his fatal fall

Breughel painted
a pastoral scene indifferent
to his tragic fall

Thresholds

Contemplating the river rushing
heedlessly onwards, I felt disheartened.
Before the river gets tainted by the undertow
new thresholds shaped by Time's storms
may become the stepping-stones
of a new awakening, I thought.

Our wiser existence celebrates
love's neophyte birth yet bliss
is tangled up with melancholy
like a carp whose bluish black pupil
slowly dissolves into the opaque sclera
by death when it reaches the light.

The requiem of dire days was quelled
and I had regained my gait with
the love filaments threaded
to my home's warmth as I was
united with my family.

Unexpectedly, news of my cousin's
death whom I had not yet had
the chance to meet in person
and his mother's deep anguish
brought tears to my eyes. Perhaps
the juvenile crows that bled
the top of my head crimson
had foretold these dearth-news.

Could this be the new threshold
I must jostle against like a baited fish
that fights the fisherman's hook
while he hauls the line-gear to himself?

The Armed Poet

The Armed Poet

*In homage to Wallace Stevens, the poet thrice armed
with faith, language, and the Law*

The language of poetry contingent on his perception
Of the sun as the sun before it become Apollo
Or even the custodian of the poet's initiation

Into an ever-changing language leaves the poet
With a paradox. Expressed in innuendos, derisions,
And metaphors, it becomes his war between the earth and sky.

A hero's death on quasi-virtual war-fields hinders his tears.
Our chrysalis-minds, double in vision, since early childhood,
Contain objects as objects and project them while, in maturity,

We reach for their metaphysics as we stand on a misty mountain.
The poet returns from the flux of the ocean and is refreshed
Within a moment's epiphany while walking among the city's

Buildings like the reflections of Blake's Jerusalem governed
By order and grace where gang warfare is a treason forsaken.
In the city, the poet loves a shapely woman as a mother eternal

Who gently conveys a laser transparency to her children
Granting them a self-burgeoning sense of reality through
Corporeal yet flawed words within the peace of a kept room.

Imagination, the poet's sublime fiction, renders the magnolia
With its fallen leaves, fresh, through childish candour. He hides
The desire of what he lacks but invents till infinity, his evasion.

The Virtual Child

In sole retreat of worldly direction
The poet loved his Lady with a guilty
Conscience and the fear of unfaithfulness
Her early death haunting him into keen
Introspection. Like a candid paper-rose
The Lady shone within her corolla
Lit with pure light. Still, the poet loved
Her other-ego, herself a concession

To Love screened by the grace of her virtue.

The virtual child pleaded Love for pity
As he passed with his Lady into Lethe.
He sublimated his unrequited Love
Into the language of sonnets, the poet's
Hope to atone for mourning and loss.

Love's Reply

World-weary, the poet returned from
His pilgrimage and longed for his absent
Other-half with his young heart whose core
He could not reach: his reason was obscured
By doubt. He was tired and confused.
In the garden, he picked a dappled autumn
Rose whose thorns hurt him. To the poet
Whose head was bent in melancholy,

Love replied: "Your heart is broken. Your other-half
Was ill. Love healed her by offering her
Your heart. Love is but a flower whose pistil
Is hidden like your own self inside your inner being
So you can abandon yourself and perceive
Your other-half as your consolation."

Introspection

With his ideal lady, tarrying in his imagination,
Love led the poet to a deep introspection.
Yet, upon her sudden death, one luminescent
Rose shone like a paper-rose, a bright light
Emanating from its creased corolla.
"You own a beautiful white rose", the poet
Said to the strained woman who repeated
His words. Subdued in thought, the poet
Still loved his lady with a dark conscience
Yet fell in love with her screened alter-ego
For her virtue, shielding her against harm.
Guilty of love with both, the virtual child-poet

In the agony of his amorous initiation
Asked Love for genuine compassion.

Art

The confession of your affair distorted my photo.
Granted, I had no recess for you, the protean child.
Against all odds I had fallen in love with you.

Like unsatisfied teens torn from their souls
We repressed our passion while you procrastinated.
Our desire was thwarted for too long, almost frozen

So you could have a wild affair with her, yet
To my amazement, you wanted me to pose
For my portrait so you could paint me.

Suture

Like a movie maker re-making an old script
Into a new movie with new characters
To spark the viewer's imagination

I left free spaces in our love sequence
For us to fill but you preferred your art
While my wound deepened like a trench.

Time became an erratic stage hung in a void.
Cast out by your family day after day
You procrastinated your affection for me.

On my birthday, you left me waiting for you
Dressed up like a pin-up while you drove away
With my best friend to visit a castle on the lake.

Like a skewed robot, I re-plunged into myself
To avoid the frustration that stifled my trust
While my breaths were trapped in my throat.

Time, the healer, offered me the gift of freedom
Like a laser distance meter that healed the suture
And restored my integrity. I could finally say "No".

The Bee's Sting
After Salvator Dali's "Sueno causado par el vuelo de una Abeja", 1944

Dali's goddess of fecundity floats
On the rock of nudity like a pomegranate
Bursting open with lucent crimson seeds.

She is dreaming of Bernini's celestial elephant,
Levitating between Dali's earth and the cerulean sky
On the lithe arachnid legs of her own wishful memory.

Now a bee buzzes inside the canvas:
A pomegranate spawns an orange fish
That begets a predatory feline suspended
In mid-air. With drawn-out claws, a tiger
Leaps towards her and touches her arm
With the surrealist painter's phallic bayonet.

Yet, still sleeping, she dreams of Bernini's Obelisk
The emblem of Dali's inspiration, his solar libido
To which she'll respond when the bee stings her breasts.

Ode to Sleep

O Sleep, descend upon me softly
And close my tired eyelids slowly.
O Sleep, let me slip into my shadow
Like a candle waning out into the night.

O Sleep, screen me off from the world's
Turmoil to create space for the new day.
O Sleep, let me forge new experiences
By memory's patina shaped by you.

O Sleep, close off my consciousness
That companion of regret that torments me.
O Sleep, protect me from bygone conflicts
And guilty remorse inflicting woe.

O Sleep, ferment my night with dreams
That satisfy my wishes with reborn desire.
O Sleep, thread my life's frayed filaments
To strengthen my stance, balance, and gait.

O Sleep, fill me with oblivion so I can sleep
Then, wake to a new life of consolation.
O Sleep, lull me with profound repose
Until I can slowly regain my soul's poise.

Quarantine

Protest

Like ant-swarms with dark beating hearts
Women advanced with a steady step along
The university park, marching through
The iron-wrought city-gates to gather slowly
Around the bronze statue of a general.
They began to protest, by turn, on a microphone
Against lean unequal salaries, short pregnancy
Breaks, lack of kindergartens, bullying
In the workplace followed by the painful mobbing.
A woman began a talk about the misogyny
Of our puritanical societies because men feared
Women, condescended and dominated them.
Then, an immigrant woman spoke on the excision
Of adolescent girls to reduce their pleasure
And all the women began to shout in protest
While another woman grabbed the mike
And said "Move on". The women picketed
In yet another city-square, marching on
To counter their contingent masculine projections,
Shielding their bodies with banners
Of equality like tough totems of fertility.

Quarantine

Plague germs steal in with the sunset
through the port into the urban arteries
through the round, hairy, curved, bony backs
by the spry tails of the panic-stricken rats.
The city is under strict quarantine.

Sisyphus, the plague's harbinger, stifles
his scapegoats' gasps under heaps
of stone where he hides his loot.

A lost automaton, Sisyphus rolls to the hill's top
the ceaseless rock of his ill-spent guilt.
Sisyphus' gyrating ghost, Black-Death-1347,
rooted out twenty-five million souls, snuffing
the vigil lights off vicars, off hamlets, off manors
in the scar of three winters. As did Covid-19.

In the city, the plagued choir-child yells out
his accursed yet cleansed guts to the white
deafness of a bed-ridden ward. Despite Sisyphus'
ghost hovering above the urban plague
the doctor gleans the boy's final scream
like a tiller who harrows, burrows,
ploughs, and plants the land.

Covid-19

A wanderer saw
the bearded vulture fly off
from the granite rock

During our confinement
we dream vividly our deep
childhood wishes

Through dreams we enter
the timeless formless optics
of the surreal soul

We dream of nebulae
sharing their twin-light among
tenebrous gas-clouds

Counterpoint

In Hogarth's forlorn night, the drunk freemason
who forbid gin in town stumbled home
through the old cobble-stones. The bonfire
in the centre burst into flames when a horse
carriage with its huge reversed wheel crushed
down on the fire, glowing like a volcano.
The fire warmed the homeless huddled
to sleep under a rough badged shelter

like new-borns in a maternity. Counterpoint.
Some terracotta dishes stood aligned on the roof's
edge containing some patients' blood like the molten
candle-wax of snuffed-out candles drawn out
by the barber-surgeon like the hair-shafts
of his client's nose. In dire curiosity, the beacon-boy
glimpses on the chaos of the fire-struck street.

The Gin Epidemic, 1751

A mother's syphilitic leg is separated from
a dying poet by the dog of despair. The skeletal
poet personifying Death, stares blindly before him
next to the printed ballad named "The downfall of Mr. Gin".

Clasping the breasts of his phlegmatic mother
with his small legs, the gin-soaked toddler topples
down the bannister to his untimely death.
The Covid-19 pandemic now sprawls

through the dark entrails of our cities
like the cocaine-crack for which passers-by
are violated for a few gratuitous wanton pounds.

In Hogarth's pawnbroker, a woman trades
her tea-pot to buy the gin that will gnaw
her vital organs like the acid that corrodes

the caustic incisions of Hogarth's etching.

Tatters

Through the tatters of our greed
the virus clung to our lungs, congested

our breath. Through our animal longings
through bats, rabbits, and pangolins

sold in hermetic blood-markets for food
and drugs, the virus clogged our vital

exchange with the world. Like the first
humans, we are barren, our frayed

clothes quarantined with disrespect.

Time's Disintegration

Will Covid-19 spread from the fish markets
into a metallic pool where we will mutate
into primordial fish while others remain above
the disintegration of Time? Will we, at last, leave
the bats, foxes, and pangolins in their own
kingdoms safe from our manipulations
to avoid Covid-19's thousand mutations?
Will we slow down our pace as in our
confinement to prevent Dali's warped Time
from turning the metallic pool into bullets? Or
will flowers mutate into plastic objects floating
on a jelly-sea of brine? Or will currents still
circulate in the oceans and clear the air
we breathe? In the post Covid-19 space
will our Time be stretched into the poem's
eternal present, allowing us transformative
change through language, rhythm, and rhyme?

The Stages of Cruelty – 1751 & 2020

While a gentleman offers a tart to stop the murderer
The dog is killed with an arrow stuck to its body
While another boy pulls on his throat with a rope.

A youngster ties a bone to another dog's tail and grins
While the dog tries to catch it. Cats are hung on a pole
And a bird's eye is cauterized with a stick as boys watch.

The sadism of Hogarth's slum-boys that turns boys
Into tyrants, in turn, makes men into poachers who murder
Pangolins and sell their scales for medicine, their meat for food.

Bitten by bats, pangolins, traded and consumed for their meat
Spread the Covid-19 virus, killing thousands by lung
Constriction, leaving the rest of us in mute confinement.

Foxes

I dreamed of a long table on a wild prairie
Strewn with snowdrops, daffodils,
Foxgloves, orchids, and eglantines.

Newcomers were offered wild flower-icons
As gifts by waiters wearing leather outfits.
Suddenly, two red foxes with white spots

Like snow drops on the tip of their tails
Approached our table and left with meat
On their mouths for the distant woods.

Scared of wild animals, some guests left
The long table, alert as the snow foxes
Darting to probe the deep snow for prey.

The Fox

In the bus, people spoke about Covid-19.
Like swarms of sardines swirling round
And round the black-blue shadow
Of the sea to reach the light, I imagined
Distant queues self-distancing in shopping
Malls before gaining the daylight outside.
In the bus, adolescents talked about
Masquerades, giggled, and laughed.
Then, unexpectedly, we heard the screeching
Brakes as the bus halted in the middle
Of a natural reserve. Through the large
Windows we saw a majestic red fox
With a fur of amber gold crossing the strait
Road in the wan winter light, its torso
And long bushy tail tainted white.
Its pointed ears and taut snout were alert.
Animals that keep a sylvan vigil in the forest
Move, hide, and hunt, sometimes uncloak
Themselves warily. Separated by a verge
From the bland gray asphalt road it traversed,
The guileful and shrewd eyes of the fox shone
Like children's agate marbles vying to target
Other marbles. Amazed at its beauty
I scrutinized the fox's heedful steps
As it entered the dark green fir forest
Heaved before us as an alpine totem.

Crows and Quills

King-like, carrion crows strutted
The streets, foraging for food, the bright
Sun turning their feathers ebony.
They had croaked loudly on the rooftops
The whole afternoon. As I walked
Along the street, two juvenile crows
Swished over my head, then flew away
And when I looked up and screamed hard
They sky-dived into my head like rockets
Bleeding me crimson. Two passers-by
Amazed by this Hitchcock-like scene,
Accompanied me home, my head covered
With my blood-tainted, white jacket.

People here feed them in the discontent
Of their unachieved raven-stories.
The vet said they would not be culled
In their breeding season due to contingency
Plans. In the safety of home, I imagined wryly
The quill-maker's hands sharpen
The quill of my revenge. I imagined
A local hunter shooting the crows
With a gun, then plucking their feathers
And cutting the barbs with his quill knife
Burning and rounding the stem-edges
To polish them incisively for the scribes.

Memorabilia
For Davide

The crows death-croaked ceaselessly.
Like a desolate flower, I shed
My pollen of salt-tears
On your painted effigy
After a truck hit your car.
I refused to believe
That you would give up your life
After a long coma wrecked
You inexorably in urgent care.
We had written letters
And I had read your legal
Translations for the newspaper
To hold their colloquia gratuitously.
Your uncanny death hindered
Our meeting face-to-face
Turning my regret to remorse –
You, gone so young, gone so pure into space
Like the emptiness the written poem leaves
In a room that contains much memorabilia.

The Bell

Like tattered flags blown by a tempest
Our link to the animal kingdom is severed
By a greed-knife sharper than the sheath
Meant to contain it. The virus that came

Through bats imprisoned in iron cages
Imprisons us, in turn. Corralled as if by water
We have become as distant archipelagos
Ignoring that each choking breath vanquishes us.

Despite Donne's warning that no man
Is an island but part of the continent
We became as islands strayed on the main

Unheeding the bell that would kill the bat
Would kill us, too, unheeding of our reciprocal
Breaths, unheeding that the bell tolls for us all.

Self-shielded

Like Perseus shielded by Medusa's
Reflection we may be shielded
By our own selves as we self-confine.

Our faces may become the mirror-shields
Of our narcissistic desires and greed.
Our imagination may overflow with protean

Fantasies that can turn against us the way
Perseus killed the Medusa with her own reflection
On his silver shield. Rendered vulnerable
By the crisis, the severed head he held is ours.

Medusa-like will we turn others into stone
In our self-isolation seeking our own blight?
Or in the tide of ripened self-reflection
Will we find our place beyond inequity?

The Trapped Rake
After Hogarth's "A Rake's Progress", Plate 7, 1763

Was the white-wigged actor prompting
his text while he supported the rake's wife
as she fainted on the prison floor
his papers dwindling beside him?

The prisoner gazed nowhere
with blank obstructed eyes
that failed to see as if a virtual
screen protected him from all
his debts while corruption, personified
by the warden, armed by a key
and a large ledger, justified
his imprisonment and extortion.

Despite his syphilitic indifference
he benefited from victimisation.

Trapped between two wives
and a beggar of alms, the prisoner
was tense like a mistreated wild dog
unable to roam. His right hand
was stretched in dire protest.
The left spelled rigid resignation.

In the microcosm of the world-stage,
a woman infused smelling salts
to the fainted wife with one closed fist
while another almost slapped her
to wake her to the ministry of the world
while all the while the actor's
angel-pennon's attire watched
the prisoners from above.

The Rake's Quarantine
After Hogarth's "A Rake's Progress", Plate 8

The madmen's keeper has his hands on the rake's
Shackled leg, the clergyman has his on the devoted wife,

A common *Pietà,* reaching for the rake's bare arm,
His bare torso exposed to the stifling light of Cibber's

Madhouse, his hand dug deep into his head's torments.
The Prodigal Son, who lost his mind to the chaos of his chains,

Is incarcerated with plague victims, shorn-haired witches
He womanized with, a forlorn fiddler, a madman

Miming the Pope, a fake scientist scribbling graffiti
On Hogarth's wall engraved with the reverse

Of a regal halfpenny that reads "Britannia/1763".

The Dream-Mask

Darkness Revisited

My mind is in fright.
The forest usurps the light.
Cougars stalk the night.

The forest hides my lover's face.
He emerges from the holt, lithe
as a wind-chafed sepia reed.

When he went wild with his tycoon
mistress, my wound succumbed
to continuous contempt.

Despite our persistent lacunae
and his nonchalant persona
we could not break up.

Is the daylight dimmed by the forest
as the witness of his cold betrayal?

A troop of travelling actors and acrobats move
into the clearing near me turning my existence
into a stage built and re-built for change.

I leave the frightening forest behind me
to contemplate the light streaming
out of the coral-clouds above the clearing.

Will the light-giver ever palliate the wound
Of betrayal lurking within the forest's darkness?

The Dream-Mask

I witnessed the cold eyes of greed
bent on money. I had ripped off the mask
from my lover's terrified face.

I recollected the hints of a forgotten dream
buried in the dunes of my memory. My lover's
face, galled by the wind, floated upon the river
that captivated him. Hard on seduction, his mask
shielded the betrayal he hid from me.

I had dreamed to reach the source
of my troubled wishes, haunting me
while I was wide-awake –

the dream warranted the passage of time
as if we navigated on a cruise ship
traversing the seas of our transience.

Like the spirit that makes us recollect
dream-cues within sleep's labyrinths
my lover's mask watched out for us
until the mask regained his face
after his disconcerting disclosure.

The Dream-Shadow

After we broke up, the cloak of forgetfulness
Wrapped me within its soft fur, lulling me to sleep.
Asleep by the river's flank, your virtual face
Appeared among the reeds, an apparition

So much resembling you, I still believe
It was the real you haunting me
While your shadow watched me sleep
And your bleak presence disturbed my dream.

Upon waking, I remembered my wound:
Like a protean child afraid to commit yourself,
You procrastinated, preferring your bird-flight
To our twin-song until we almost fell apart.

Come, my love, let's now restore
The frayed filaments of our lost love.
Come, my love, let's stitch our tattered attires
Into a fabric patterned by our desire.

The Eastern Façade

Like an anchoress, I walked along the corridor
Of the newly built country cottage on the eastern façade.
While I gazed at the unfinished rooms, the dank smell

Of the humid cement-binder on the brick walls haunted
My eerie dream. Then, there appeared a long bar
Where I waited with a friend to order food.

The waiter neglected us so we walked away.
Seated, we spoke about our new fluid maturity
That assumed hunger and loss like a new life

Purified of its past wounds, gleaning new growth.
Finally, we were served food and beer. While the effluvium
Of the humid concrete still suffused my nose, I resumed

My tour of the unachieved eastern house, the tang
Of the damp cement-binder still titillating my nose
While my waking body moored memories to words.

The Hawk's Prey

A sudden flap of white wings against
the twilight, wide as the car's trajectory
rent our talk on translations and meanings.
The hawk drew an ellipse in the sky
a brown mammal clutched in its outstretched
claws hunted as it hunts the fish and the frog.
The predator's meal was to be eaten within
the barn-beams wooden intimacy.

Could the owl's dark hunt be as guiltless
and clean as the skills of its prey?
Through what dark design did the hawk
extract the small mammal from the architecture
of its burrow built with exits for its offspring
like bunkers for the soldiers of the great war?

Trammel

In the clearing, hunters hidden behind
bush-shelters dug a dozen duck decoys
in deep mud, imitated their cries and songs
then shot them. Ducks fell one by one
through tricks, lures, and alloys.
An eagle snatched a falling prey.

The sculptor chose exquisite cedar
wood to sculpt a duck: the wings
were chiseled, striated, and painted
in iridescent green while the body
was shaped with burgundy redwood.
The eyes made of dark glass beads
contrasted with the large orange beak.

May we hear the snow yield
to the sage and the sweet saxifrage
as the pewter gong heralds an era
of pastoral care like a deep-set mirror
of recognition that values art
rather than the killer-decoy.

Triassic Gifts

I exercise my legs, counting to ten –
Twenty – thirty – forty – then, begin
Swimming back and forth and back again
Towards the long glass windows, now
Disclosing a congregation of chamois
bouncing and gamboling on the rocks.
I feel weightless as a feather in the wind.

The mountain's triassic water relaxes
My tense sinews. The wondrous water
Feels like baptism on my body
As I immerse myself in the pool
Charged with iron, calcium,
Magnesium, salt, and fluoride.

I now see the snow-capped slopes through
The large windows and at a closer look
Discern huge pine cones trailing on the tall
Tenebrous larches like breasts of abundance.

The next morning, a howling icy wind spiraled
Hail and snow on the windows, swirling the snow
From the rooftops, bending the tall pines.

On the mountain

Ravens stretch their beaks
to reach the sunflowers
on the balcony

With the first new snow
the mountains sleep, hidden
in the morning mist

A huge hunter moon
lights the winter sky like
a nocturnal lamp

The north wind bends pines
whirls and sweeps snow from the roofs
the night sky turns blue

The Ascent

Without warning, the pumice from Vesuvius
Engulfed Pompeii like a sudden burst
Of inspiration. As we climbed up, the trail's
Ferruginous soil moved under my shoes
Until we reached the summit under the kiln-sun.
On the caldera, I thought of the erotic frescoes
That purified the bedrooms – the swan-god
Encroached on Leda's body, Sappho
With her pen warning us of the cataclysm.
The frescoes that survived the refined city
Purged by fire and ash are the tragic reminders
Of mores and dreams like inklings of poems
Wrought into sonnets that rise above
The house-rubble of the unconscious.

Transience

I dreamed of an immobile train
like a static reptilian in the mist.
The dream moved on and in the train's
restaurant, I spoke with a young man
reading "In Search of Lost Time".

We spoke of the madeleine moment,
how the cake must have slowly melted
in Swann's mouth, sugar euphorizing
his young mind like a drug. The dream,
then, moved on to my childhood anorexia –

my refusal to eat unless engaged
in play with my grandmother on the beach
with buckets and rakes. I would begin to eat
when the pebbles started skimming on the sea-skin.

As the dream moved on,
the young man and I spoke
of how the cycles of hunger fluctuated
like the earth-cycles girdled
by the sun, cycles shifting
with the earth's magnetic attraction
to the sun like lovers moving close
and then apart, then, by turn of tide,
together again tied by transience.

Pentimento

Upon Pegasus we rode, silk-wings
Transparent against the moonlight
The mirror of our anguish and flight.
The night trembled with new-born terror

While you dreamed of the dread lurking
In disguise in the obscure frameless forest
And suffered from the blind increment
Of bile you could not contain. Our excess

Desire quelled into an unrequited love
Became locked in this irregular sonnet
And subdued our anguish in its stanzas

As from the white *pentimento* page
A hundred starlings took their flight
In our perpetual daydreams to alight.

The Dream Cadence

Lost in a wild forest where rivers ran
At counter cadence, I could not step
Into the river of my dream. Each clue
Was immediately swept away by the original
Dream that kept slipping away. Did I walk
On an open field or was I celebrating
A victory? I do not know. The failed dream

Escaped me. As Zephyr slowly dispersed
My sadness, I reconstructed a virtual dream
To soothe my melancholy. The real dream
Was memory's offspring that restored my breath.
It was a wish fulfilled and the poem's palimpsest.

Like the north star that leads the nocturnal way
The accomplished dream palliates the day.

Inscape

Inscape

Treading the wild moors for miles
A solitary figure gathered leeches
That would sting sick bodies, purge
Their blood, cleanse, and cure them.
Like the leech-gatherer who refused
To relinquish his quest and assert
His self-reliance, I walked relentlessly
Upon the sand dunes to reach the sea.

On the beryl-beach, I floated on the primal
Waters like a swift marine animal defying
Gravity. Water, abundant with iron and iodine
Released my breathing and vitalized me.

Tasting the salty sea-plasma, I felt
Complete and secure with earthly joy.
In my spirit's independence, I swam
Towards the horizon, floating upon
The oceanic billow, my body bound
To the ocean's song, each liquid atom
Binding me to mankind. Like the leech
Gatherer's heather the sea tamed
By my stout swimming body
Became a harmony of inscape
A recognition generating poetry.

The Scantling
After Breughel's "The Procession to Calvary", 1564

Peasants danced in reels while his pregnant wife shed
Bitter tears of grief mingled with the vultures' shrieks.

Like a martyr, crucified in imitation of Christ,
Breughel painted the young shepherd shorn

From his pasture and tied to the wheel hoisted
Outside town as the scantling of the heathens.

He painted the town's rich politicians costumed
In silk brocades, silent in their Janus-like hypocrisy

That kept the mill turning at dawn, grinding its grains
For the bread of the believers baked by bitter blood.

The Blood-Pearl
A dream vision

Conscious of imminent social change, I traversed
The Styx with Elizabeth Browning. Her lyrical voice
Shaped by determination became the consolation
Bounding me to profound love and prompted me

To continue my journey between the spry earth
And the vast sky wherein flowed a translucent
Stream. In contemplation, I saw a single pearl
Tainted by a bright crimson drop of blood

Whose weight tarnished my awakening
With amplified patterns of anguish and awe.
After waking, warped nerves harrowed me

Galling my legs by electrical impulses.
My scratched skin itched, chafing my blood
Like a river-bed scraped by stones and grit.

On the Causeway

The delta-fields under my feet
spurted into myriad twin orchid rows
after the seeding. I walked upon a long
causeway where the river's umber alluvium
oozed into the cobalt sea languidly
as in rising dough, reminding me
of the wind-swept, shape-shifting
sepia sands moving among the dunes.

As I walked along, the day's draught
scorched my skin when I, suddenly, heard
a flock of swifts migrating to a desert
abundant in ants, locusts, and scorpions.
I saw their swarms in rhythms of evolving
flight in fledgling patterns to avoid predators.

They were imprinted with sequels of subdued
ancestral wisdom like the shaping spirit
brooding in the poem, linking metaphors,
the articulate syntax boosting our memory.

Birthright
A Trespass

The wild hunter was hungry.
He hunted the bear and the antelope
In the wilderness. On impulse, he renounced
His birthright for a lentil stew to his twin brother.

Disguised in sheepskin, his twin personified him
And stole the blessed inheritance. The hunter strayed
From home, herding the animals of his in-laws
But was, later, cast out for fraudulent ownership.

Weary from roaming, the hunter realized
That he would carry the yoke of his impudence
Through the land until he abandoned his trespass.

Conceding to his brother's mild hierarchy,
He consented to the creed of his patriarchy.

Transformations

The sun plays hide-and-seek with
the light in the orchard bursting
with sweet nectar the salmon-velvet
peaches ready for the new harvest.

Like pink diamonds deftly cut, shaped
and polished by jeweler-hands
dew drops scintillate on the clustered
corollas of the silk mimosas.

Sunlight shines on the caterpillars feeding
on the mulberry leaves for the energy
that will transform their tender frames
into diaphanous butterflies.

Like the electrical circuits lighting up
our cities, my imagination ignites
my insight, the poem's wellspring,
and unites me with an ideal alchemy.

Self-image

The adolescent
who kept pressing
her phone button
to capture herself
automatically
actually answered
the Sphinx's riddle
about man's transition from
youth to maturity and old age.
In her quest of identity
she asserted
her fugue of freedom
unaware of the phone
as a mask between her
and her image, a mask
between childhood
and adolescence
naïvely unaware
that the image can cleave
the feigned from the real.

The Olive Branch

Like the perennial promise
Of the vital olive oil proffered
By millennial olive trees
I discerned an olive branch
Protruding from a brick wall
On the avenue where I walked.

The Minotaur-Daughter
After L. Carrington's painting, 1953

Ocular glass balls tumble down in disarray
On the floor like the taboo-apples from Eve's
Tree of knowledge into the orchard-garden
When Eden's primal scene was interrupted.

The candid game between the dead barren
Nun-Mother and the satyr's ludic libido grabble
Down the velvet tablecloth near a fallen rose.

The children sneak into the naughty ball game
Their mother plays with her Nun-Mother's ghost,
A lithe flower-figure with a *fleur-de-lys* attached
On her sharp scapula, a domineering figure.

The elder, wrapped in his black cloak
Seems amused by the foolish young satyr
But his younger brother, disconcerted
And in austere scrutiny stares defiantly
At his anthropomorphic mother.

The Minotaur-Daughter

His skillful bare hands stand free
In tender appeal. Both are cautious
Both curious, both afraid of their mother's
Magnified imagined trinity.

I dreamed of a white patriarchal satyr
Disguised as the wild minotaur's daughter.
Surprised by her sons, the satyr
Became her father's foil.

Her hands were suddenly startled.
Her horned torso gleefully faced
The dogs guarding her hidden
Dancing body crowned by a sapling.

Her erotic nudity was shadowed
By Carrington to protect her young
Children from straying for now they
Would prolong their maternal trinity.

Epithalamium

Like a newly-wed bride trailing her silk dress,
The veiled mountain strewn with winter snow
Unfolds in the mist of the early afternoon.

Like diamonds scattered in the moss, the arcane
Day sparkles as if under an alchemist's dome
Of quintessence to shelter the lovers in the play.

The errant caravan in the clearing stages
"A Midsummer Night's Dream" with the fairies
Playing impish tricks to echo the lovers' folly.

Puck suddenly spots Cupid's aphrodisiac to lure
And mismatch the couples with the nymphs' hymns
Then steals the lovers' masks and flees.

The fairies' masks safeguard their desires
As they blend with the forest and the waters
To revel unhindered like sylvan spirits.

Now the lovers take on the fairy-masks
To protect their romance and embrace in liberty
As they lose themselves in the forest's tapestry.

While the Satyrs lust, the wedding chords
Resonate in the electrified air and we still stay
Beguiled with magical lures and love legends.

Rebellion With An Actor and A Poet

I met an unknown actor by the river
reciting Blake's "Songs of Innocence
and Experience". He had returned
from the river's congested mouth
in turmoil like the sacrificial sea.

Kingfish-refugees gathered
on the beach, around bonfires
waiting to end their life-risk on land.

The migrants were more vulnerable
than even migrating birds, a chorus
led to their rightful destinations
by millenary magnetic patterns.

Innocent like blades of grass
their children were lost, severed
from their parents, trapped
in lands of cruel egotism.

At last, the actor facing
the blood-sea, scarlet
with migrant gore, rebelled
and recited Blake's paradox:

"Pity would be no more
If we did not make somebody poor."

And the sea replied with Blake's voice:
"Then cherish pity, lest you drive an angel from your door."

Water On Water

I. Hypnotic Zero

Like Fabergé's hypnotic bird, I glide
on a turquoise water-field shifting
with the sunlight. The water recycles
itself, confining the shore's elegy
inside a convex water drop reminding me
of the lethargy of my dead mother's
lead-seas, a stifling immobility
land-shielded by wrath
hollow upon me.

Breathing in, breathing out
until hypnotic zero

II. The Water-Dirge

Zephyr's breath stirs the sea-skin as glaciers shrink
into pounded grit and icebergs swamp the shores.

    Salt is oozed from the sea-water by tongues
of thirst while we lament the mourning seas.

III. Migration

with the swallows, I flew out.
with others, I descended
into the taboo-zone
where water's immanence
was censured ......by babies' cries
by subsided water-bourns
and electronic sirens
shrieking their grief
in the black hole of wrath.

IV. Mirth

like soldiers landing on the D-day beaches
the ire of the waves smite the shoreline

yet sea-sentinels still restore the protean
shore while cerulean currents stream

beneath the swell where the plankton abounds
and sperm whales sing with the sea's rhythm

until circular crotchets close the water-cycle.

The New Order

The minotaur is captive in the poem's labyrinth.
The beast feeding on sacrificial human flesh
Will only forsake his prey when the poet's torments
Subside like the weakening ill wind that sinks ships.

Until then, the beast must pace within the maze
Trying to figure out his escape. The king believes
Human sacrifice protects the harbor and his ships
Yet he cannot deal with the minotaur's savagery

Nor the poet's life-force that sustains the text.
Like the ingenious Ariadne, the poet unravels
The thread leading out of the labyrinth to save

Regal Theseus who will slay the savage beast.
The sonnet's turn points to an order of courage
That defeats the price of human sacrifice.

The Clash of Contraries
After William Blake

Like the poet whose kingdom is projection
Cleansing the windows of our perception
I scrape the scourge off men's faces
And etch their faces on copper plates.
One day, the face of a broken refugee
Appeared smudged by blood and tears.
I said: "The sea is etched on your skin.
    Wipe the water off your chest and
    Do not look back if expelled."

Plate I
Reversal of Truth

I visited Blake's printing house in the Red Cross
Where, in narrow lines, prisoners' files are aligned
Within archives suspended on grey war-chains
Their Fate sealed with death or the unknown.
There were names after names of lost souls
Of unexchanged prisoners since war rules
Remained unchanged and the treatment
Of prisoners was ignored in wartime.

Plate II
Time's Archives

Man's weltered memory registers the traces of invasions
Stalked buffer-zones to be rebuilt, refugee camps enlarged
Where memory is countered and oppressed by conmen.
Knowledge is suppressed over the generations
Power perverted by a Janus-headed bureaucracy
Spreading like cancer. Somnolent archives are consulted
To reach a consensus for the resolution of contraries
Against pedophiles, illegal migration, and human trafficking
Through education and humanitarian law against war.

Plate III
Science Built on Man's Guilt

Like a hunter slaying a tiger, man survives
Though the sublimated guilt that built science
At the expense of apes, monkeys, or prisoners
Mishandled for profit which caused the pandemic.
If we repudiate this, we hold a match against the sun
Towards orphaned earth, an offering to death,
Like a wounded babe deprived of gratified desire.

Plate IV
The Eagle and the Ox

Can an Empire soar despite the eagle's sovereign brutality?
For the poet, the kingdom of poetry is insight
Winnowing through our five senses, our sources of energy.
The ox of reason tempers our excess desire
Protecting us from unnecessary nightmares.
Yet, hungry priests reave men of natural myths
Neutralizing Nature to frighten us with speculations.
The rule for the eagle and the ox is oppression.

Plate V
The Cassini Probe

Cassini probes Saturn's methane moons
Plunges into its storm-ridden atmosphere
Through the largest gap between its rings.
It scans photos of the water-plumes, jutting
From Titan's ocean-girth, celebrating
The music of its garnered rings radiant in space.
A woman astronomer on a space mission,
I polish the windows of our perception
So we can all regain acuity and the world liberty.

Acknowledgements

"Quarantine" first appeared in my book, *A Woman By A Well*, Matador Books, 2015

"Art", "Water on Water", "Birthright", and "The Clash of Contraries", the latter published in *Journal of Poetics Research*, first appeared in my book, *The Threshold of Broken Waters*, Matador Books, 2018

"Ravens…" in *Three Line Poetry*, Issue 50, November 2018

"Vigilance" in *Literary Heist*, Spring Issue, March 21, 2019

"The Olive Branch" in *The Expanded Field Literary Journal*, Vrije University in Amsterdam, Issue 4, March 29, 2019

"The Dream-Mask (I)", "Unrequited" or "Pentimento" in *Oxford School of Poetry Review*, April 2019 https://www.oxfordschoolofpoetry.com/osp-review

"Fluctuations" in *Synaeresis*, Issue 7, April 2019. https://issuu.com/harmoniapress/docs/synaeresis_issue_seven

"Ultrasound" in *Subterranean Blue Poetry*, Volume VII, Issue IX, October 2019

"The Minotaur-Daughter" in *San Antonio Review*, September 1st, 2019

"Triassic Gifts" in *Halcyon Days*, Issue 15, September 2019

"The Dream-Shadow" in *Tipton Poetry Journal*, Issue 42, October 2019

"Foxes" in *Erothanatos*, Literary Journal of Calcutta University, Vol. 3 Issue 4, October 20, 2019

"The Blood-Pearl," "Introspection", and "On the Causeway" in *E.ratio*, Issue 29, January 1st, 2020

"The New Order" in The Blue Nib", Issue 40, January 2020

"Rebellion with An Actor and A Poet", in *Impspired*, January 2020 https://impspired.com/2019/11/25/bilman-e-emily-bilman/

"The Water-Shadow" in *Breadcrumb* No. 565, February 18, 2020

"The Virtual Child" in *Poetica Review*, Issue 5, Spring 2020

"Transience" in *The Green Light Journal*, June 1st, 2020

"Inscape" and "The Torn Tower" in *Wild Court*, June 22, 2020

"Time's Disintegration" and "Stages of Cruelty – 1751 & 2020" in *North of Oxford* – The Pandemic Issue #4 https://northofoxford.wordpress.com/2020/04/27/north-of-oxford-the-pandemic-issue-4/

"Trammel", "The Dream Cadence", "Trapped Rake", in *Trouvaille Review*, May 16, 2020 https://www.trouvaillereview.org/

"The Rake's Quarantine, Plate 8", "Protest", "The Child and The Prism" in *Otherwise Engaged*, Volume 5, The Quarantine Edition, Summer 2020

"Transformations" in Offshoots 15, September 2020

"Thresholds" in ExTempore, United Nations Magazine, Winter 2020

"Apperception", "The Armed Poet", "The Gin Epidemic 1751", "Counterpoint" in *The Blue Nib*, June 13, 2020 https://thebluenib.com/4-poems-by-emily-bilman/

"The Fox" Birdsong, June 15, 2020 https://birdsongjournal.blogspot.com/

"The Bee's Sting" in San Antonio Review, July 5, 2020 https://sa-review.com/2020/poetry/emilybilman/2277/

"Tatters" in Eighteen Seventy, July 8, 2020. https://eighteenseventy.poetry.blog/2020/07/08/tatters-by-emilie-bilman/

"Self-shielded" in Nine Clouds Journal, Issue One, August 2020

"The Life-Buoy and The Blackbird", "Ode to Sleep" in Praxis Magazine, Nigeria, August 11, 2020

"The Bell", Newsletter of the Poetry Society of Virginia, USA, September 2020

Author's Biography

Dr. Emily Bilman is London's Poetry Society Stanza representative in Geneva. Her doctoral dissertation, *The Psychodynamics of Poetry: Poetic Virtuality and Oedipal Sublimation in the Poetry of T.S. Eliot and Paul Valéry* was published by Lambert Academic in 2010 and *Modern Ekphrasis* by Peter Lang in 2013. In her thesis, she demonstrates her concept of "creative virtuality" through which poets assume an objective virtual persona to write about trauma. Her poetry books, *A Woman By A Well* (2015), *Resilience* (2015), and *The Threshold of Broken Waters* (2018) were published by Troubador, UK. Her essay, "T.S. Eliot's Combined Personae as Tiresias-Narcissus in The Waste Land", was published in The Battersea Review no. 5 in 2015. "*Geoffrey Hill's Poetry and The Phenomenology of the Non-Self*" appeared in *The Journal of Poetics Research* JPR06 in March 2017 and "*Plath Riding Into Thanatos*" in *Twelve Rivers*, Vol. 11 in May 2020. Her poems were published in *The London Magazine, Poetry Salzburg Review, Offshoots, San Antonio Review, Expanded Field, Journal of Poetics Research, The Blue Nib, Poetica Review, Tipton Poetry Journal, North of Oxford Journal, Trouvaille Review, Three Line Poetry, Wild Court,* etc.
She blogs on http://www.emiliebilman.wix.com/emily-bilman